voiceJunction

SATB (with SAT semi-chorus) and cello

OXFORD

Sarah Quartel

Ripple Effect

Texts and translation

Karitas habundat in omnia.

Love abounds in all.

Hildegard of Bingen (1098–1179)

We ourselves feel that what we are doing is just a drop in the ocean. But if that drop was not in the ocean, I think the ocean would be less because of that missing drop.

Mother Teresa (1910–97)

Commissioned by the Avanti Chamber Singers, Artistic Director Rachel Rensink-Hoff,
for 'Ripple Effect', a collaborative project with cellist and sound engineer Kirk Starkey

Ripple Effect

Hildegard of Bingen (1098–1179)
Mother Teresa (1910–97)

SARAH QUARTEL

* The repeated word 'Love' is always sung for the duration of the slurred phrase, using an 'ah' vowel, and placing the final consonant 'v' on the rest at the end of the phrase, as shown.

Duration: 5.5 mins

OXFORD UNIVERSITY PRESS, MUSIC DEPARTMENT, GREAT CLARENDON STREET, OXFORD OX2 6DP

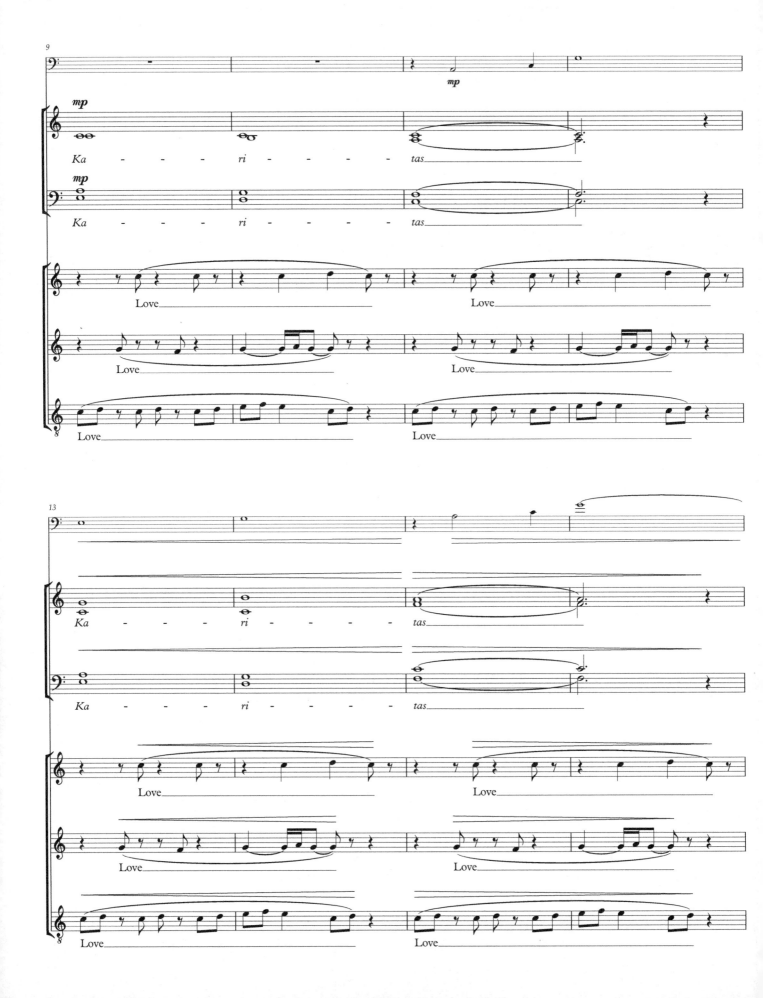

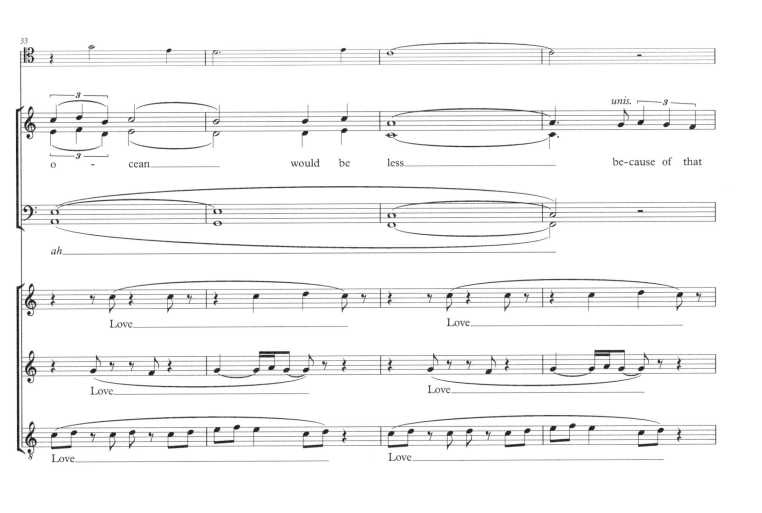

o - cean_____ would be less_____ be-cause of that

ah_____

Love_____

Love_____

Love_____

miss-ing drop._____

Love_____

Love_____

Love_____

12

* see note on first page of music

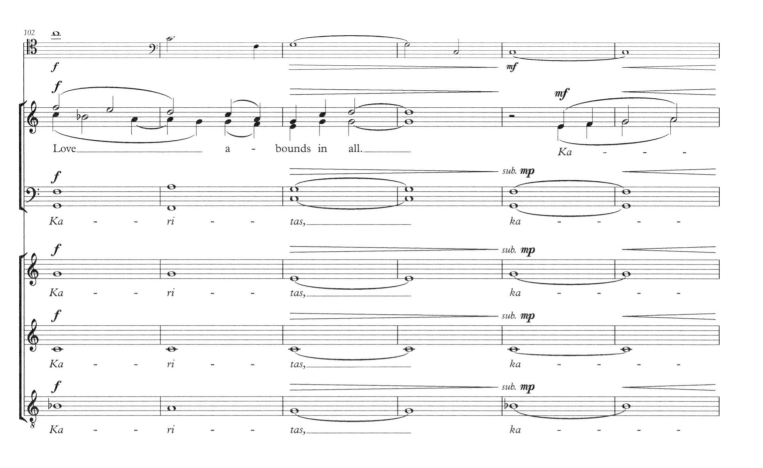

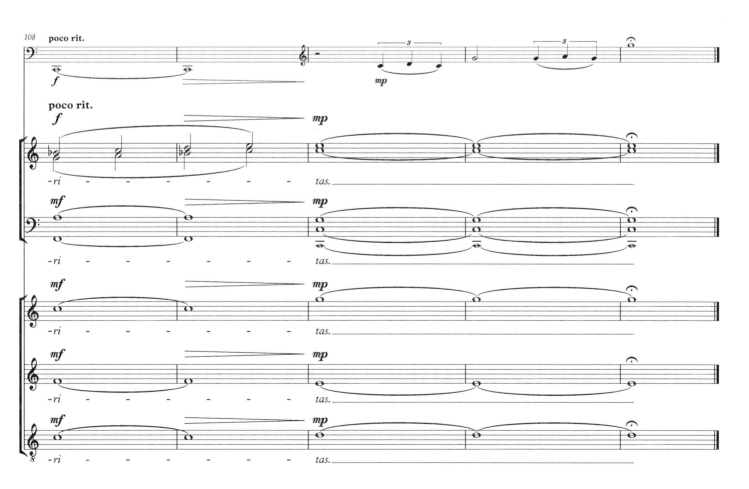

Ripple Effect

SARAH QUARTEL

Printed in Great Britain

Music origination by Julia Bovee

voiceJunction

Voice Junction is an inspirational series of secular songs for all modern mixed-voice singing groups. A meeting point of various styles, the series is fresh, popular, and alternative in feel, and includes new original works—both accompanied and *a cappella*—alongside unique arrangements of well-known tunes. Whether performed by a one-per-part vocal group or a community choir, this is music that brings people together.

Sarah Quartel is a Canadian composer and educator known for her fresh and exciting approach to choral music. She celebrates the musical potential of all learners by providing singers access to engaging repertoire and transformative musical experiences. Deeply inspired by the life-changing relationships that can occur while making choral music, Sarah writes in a way that connects singer to singer, ensemble to conductor, and performer to audience. Although she has been a full-time composer since 2017, Sarah chooses to remain connected to her past as a music educator and is a guest teacher in her hometown of London, Canada. Sarah continues to work as a clinician and conductor at music education and choral events at home and abroad.

Photo: Sandra Dufton Photography

ISBN 978-0-19-356298-1

9 780193 562981

www.oup.com